Welcome
On Board

. . . .

Boaters Log Book

Have fun using this log book.

Keep track of basic boat maintenance. When you last filled up, emptied out and topped up.

Log your journeys as you cruise the cut. Make notes of your favourite stop-offs, mooring points and essential service points along your route.

Take it slowly and enjoy the journey.

This log book has been designed and created by Brett Sirrell
If you have any recommendations for future editions please drop us an email. Brett@amazingmagic.uk
If you enjoy this book please leave a review on Amazon.

Copyright Amazing Press© All rights reserved. This book or any portion thereof may not be reproduced or used in any manner whatsoever without the express written permission of the publisher.

Maintenance and Services Log

Service	Date	Notes

Maintenance and Services Log

Service	Date	Notes

Maintenance and Services Log

Service	Date	Notes

Maintenance and Services Log

Service	Date	Notes

Maintenance and Services Log

Service	Date	Notes

Maintenance and Services Log

Service	Date	Notes

Date	Departure	Arrival
Location		
Time		
Fuel		
Engine Hours		

Journey Summary			
Locks		**Air Temp**	
Swing Bridges		**Wind**	
Flow		**Rain**	

Waypoints & Stop-offs		
Location	Time	Notes

Date	Departure	Arrival
Location		
Time		
Fuel		
Engine Hours		

Journey Summary			
Locks		Air Temp	
Swing Bridges		Wind	
Flow		Rain	

Waypoints & Stop-offs		
Location	Time	Notes

	Departure	Arrival
Date		
Location		
Time		
Fuel		
Engine Hours		

Journey Summary			
Locks		Air Temp	
Swing Bridges		Wind	
Flow		Rain	

Waypoints & Stop-offs		
Location	Time	Notes

	Departure	Arrival
Date		
Location		
Time		
Fuel		
Engine Hours		

Journey Summary			
Locks		Air Temp	
Swing Bridges		Wind	
Flow		Rain	

Waypoints & Stop-offs		
Location	Time	Notes

	Departure	Arrival
Date		
Location		
Time		
Fuel		
Engine Hours		

Journey Summary				
Locks		Air Temp		
Swing Bridges		Wind		
Flow		Rain		

Waypoints & Stop-offs		
Location	Time	Notes

Date	Departure	Arrival
Location		
Time		
Fuel		
Engine Hours		

Journey Summary			
Locks		Air Temp	
Swing Bridges		Wind	
Flow		Rain	

Waypoints & Stop-offs		
Location	Time	Notes

Date	Departure	Arrival
Location		
Time		
Fuel		
Engine Hours		

Journey Summary			
Locks		Air Temp	
Swing Bridges		Wind	
Flow		Rain	

Waypoints & Stop-offs		
Location	Time	Notes

Date	Departure	Arrival
Location		
Time		
Fuel		
Engine Hours		

Journey Summary			
Locks		Air Temp	
Swing Bridges		Wind	
Flow		Rain	

Waypoints & Stop-offs		
Location	Time	Notes

Date	Departure	Arrival
Location		
Time		
Fuel		
Engine Hours		

Journey Summary			
Locks		Air Temp	
Swing Bridges		Wind	
Flow		Rain	

Waypoints & Stop-offs		
Location	Time	Notes

Date	Departure	Arrival
Location		
Time		
Fuel		
Engine Hours		

Journey Summary			
Locks		Air Temp	
Swing Bridges		Wind	
Flow		Rain	

Waypoints & Stop-offs		
Location	Time	Notes

Date	Departure	Arrival
Location		
Time		
Fuel		
Engine Hours		

Journey Summary			
Locks		Air Temp	
Swing Bridges		Wind	
Flow		Rain	

Waypoints & Stop-offs		
Location	Time	Notes

	Departure	Arrival
Date		
Location		
Time		
Fuel		
Engine Hours		

Journey Summary			
Locks		**Air Temp**	
Swing Bridges		**Wind**	
Flow		**Rain**	

Waypoints & Stop-offs		
Location	**Time**	**Notes**

Date	Departure	Arrival
Location		
Time		
Fuel		
Engine Hours		

Journey Summary			
Locks		Air Temp	
Swing Bridges		Wind	
Flow		Rain	

Waypoints & Stop-offs		
Location	Time	Notes

Date	Departure	Arrival
Location		
Time		
Fuel		
Engine Hours		

Journey Summary			
Locks		Air Temp	
Swing Bridges		Wind	
Flow		Rain	

Waypoints & Stop-offs		
Location	Time	Notes

Date	Departure	Arrival
Location		
Time		
Fuel		
Engine Hours		

Journey Summary			
Locks		Air Temp	
Swing Bridges		Wind	
Flow		Rain	

Waypoints & Stop-offs		
Location	Time	Notes

Date	Departure	Arrival
Location		
Time		
Fuel		
Engine Hours		

Journey Summary			
Locks		Air Temp	
Swing Bridges		Wind	
Flow		Rain	

Waypoints & Stop-offs		
Location	Time	Notes

Date	Departure	Arrival
Location		
Time		
Fuel		
Engine Hours		

Journey Summary			
Locks		Air Temp	
Swing Bridges		Wind	
Flow		Rain	

Waypoints & Stop-offs		
Location	Time	Notes

	Departure	Arrival
Date		
Location		
Time		
Fuel		
Engine Hours		

Journey Summary			
Locks		Air Temp	
Swing Bridges		Wind	
Flow		Rain	

Waypoints & Stop-offs		
Location	Time	Notes

Date	Departure	Arrival
Location		
Time		
Fuel		
Engine Hours		

Journey Summary			
Locks		Air Temp	
Swing Bridges		Wind	
Flow		Rain	

Waypoints & Stop-offs		
Location	Time	Notes

	Departure	Arrival
Date		
Location		
Time		
Fuel		
Engine Hours		

Journey Summary			
Locks		Air Temp	
Swing Bridges		Wind	
Flow		Rain	

Waypoints & Stop-offs		
Location	Time	Notes

Date	Departure	Arrival
Location		
Time		
Fuel		
Engine Hours		

Journey Summary			
Locks		Air Temp	
Swing Bridges		Wind	
Flow		Rain	

Waypoints & Stop-offs		
Location	Time	Notes

Date	Departure	Arrival
Location		
Time		
Fuel		
Engine Hours		

Journey Summary			
Locks		Air Temp	
Swing Bridges		Wind	
Flow		Rain	

Waypoints & Stop-offs		
Location	Time	Notes

Date	Departure	Arrival
Location		
Time		
Fuel		
Engine Hours		

Journey Summary			
Locks		Air Temp	
Swing Bridges		Wind	
Flow		Rain	

Waypoints & Stop-offs		
Location	Time	Notes

	Departure	Arrival
Date		
Location		
Time		
Fuel		
Engine Hours		

Journey Summary			
Locks		Air Temp	
Swing Bridges		Wind	
Flow		Rain	

Waypoints & Stop-offs		
Location	Time	Notes

Date	Departure	Arrival
Location		
Time		
Fuel		
Engine Hours		

Journey Summary			
Locks		Air Temp	
Swing Bridges		Wind	
Flow		Rain	

Waypoints & Stop-offs		
Location	Time	Notes

	Departure	Arrival
Date		
Location		
Time		
Fuel		
Engine Hours		

Journey Summary			
Locks		Air Temp	
Swing Bridges		Wind	
Flow		Rain	

Waypoints & Stop-offs		
Location	Time	Notes

	Departure	Arrival
Date		
Location		
Time		
Fuel		
Engine Hours		

Journey Summary			
Locks		Air Temp	
Swing Bridges		Wind	
Flow		Rain	

Waypoints & Stop-offs		
Location	Time	Notes

Date	Departure	Arrival
Location		
Time		
Fuel		
Engine Hours		

Journey Summary			
Locks		Air Temp	
Swing Bridges		Wind	
Flow		Rain	

Waypoints & Stop-offs		
Location	Time	Notes

Date	Departure	Arrival
Location		
Time		
Fuel		
Engine Hours		

Journey Summary			
Locks		Air Temp	
Swing Bridges		Wind	
Flow		Rain	

Waypoints & Stop-offs		
Location	Time	Notes

Date	Departure	Arrival
Location		
Time		
Fuel		
Engine Hours		

Journey Summary			
Locks		Air Temp	
Swing Bridges		Wind	
Flow		Rain	

Waypoints & Stop-offs		
Location	Time	Notes

Date	Departure	Arrival
Location		
Time		
Fuel		
Engine Hours		

Journey Summary			
Locks		Air Temp	
Swing Bridges		Wind	
Flow		Rain	

Waypoints & Stop-offs		
Location	Time	Notes

	Departure	Arrival
Date		
Location		
Time		
Fuel		
Engine Hours		

Journey Summary			
Locks		Air Temp	
Swing Bridges		Wind	
Flow		Rain	

Waypoints & Stop-offs		
Location	Time	Notes

	Departure	Arrival
Date		
Location		
Time		
Fuel		
Engine Hours		

Journey Summary			
Locks		Air Temp	
Swing Bridges		Wind	
Flow		Rain	

Waypoints & Stop-offs		
Location	Time	Notes

	Departure	Arrival
Date		
Location		
Time		
Fuel		
Engine Hours		

Journey Summary			
Locks		Air Temp	
Swing Bridges		Wind	
Flow		Rain	

Waypoints & Stop-offs		
Location	Time	Notes

Date	Departure	Arrival
Location		
Time		
Fuel		
Engine Hours		

Journey Summary			
Locks		Air Temp	
Swing Bridges		Wind	
Flow		Rain	

Waypoints & Stop-offs		
Location	Time	Notes

	Departure	Arrival
Date		
Location		
Time		
Fuel		
Engine Hours		

Journey Summary			
Locks		Air Temp	
Swing Bridges		Wind	
Flow		Rain	

Waypoints & Stop-offs		
Location	Time	Notes

	Departure	Arrival
Date		
Location		
Time		
Fuel		
Engine Hours		

Journey Summary				
Locks			Air Temp	
Swing Bridges			Wind	
Flow			Rain	

Waypoints & Stop-offs		
Location	Time	Notes

Date	Departure	Arrival
Location		
Time		
Fuel		
Engine Hours		

Journey Summary			
Locks		Air Temp	
Swing Bridges		Wind	
Flow		Rain	

Waypoints & Stop-offs		
Location	Time	Notes

Date	Departure	Arrival
Location		
Time		
Fuel		
Engine Hours		

Journey Summary			
Locks		Air Temp	
Swing Bridges		Wind	
Flow		Rain	

Waypoints & Stop-offs		
Location	Time	Notes

Date	Departure	Arrival
Location		
Time		
Fuel		
Engine Hours		

Journey Summary			
Locks		Air Temp	
Swing Bridges		Wind	
Flow		Rain	

Waypoints & Stop-offs		
Location	Time	Notes

Date	Departure	Arrival
Location		
Time		
Fuel		
Engine Hours		

Journey Summary			
Locks		Air Temp	
Swing Bridges		Wind	
Flow		Rain	

Waypoints & Stop-offs		
Location	Time	Notes

	Departure	Arrival
Date		
Location		
Time		
Fuel		
Engine Hours		

Journey Summary				
Locks		Air Temp		
Swing Bridges		Wind		
Flow		Rain		

Waypoints & Stop-offs		
Location	Time	Notes

Date	Departure	Arrival
Location		
Time		
Fuel		
Engine Hours		

Journey Summary			
Locks		Air Temp	
Swing Bridges		Wind	
Flow		Rain	

Waypoints & Stop-offs		
Location	Time	Notes

	Departure	Arrival
Date		
Location		
Time		
Fuel		
Engine Hours		

Journey Summary			
Locks		Air Temp	
Swing Bridges		Wind	
Flow		Rain	

Waypoints & Stop-offs		
Location	Time	Notes

	Departure	Arrival
Date		
Location		
Time		
Fuel		
Engine Hours		

Journey Summary

Locks		Air Temp	
Swing Bridges		Wind	
Flow		Rain	

Waypoints & Stop-offs

Location	Time	Notes

Date	Departure	Arrival
Location		
Time		
Fuel		
Engine Hours		

Journey Summary			
Locks		Air Temp	
Swing Bridges		Wind	
Flow		Rain	

Waypoints & Stop-offs		
Location	Time	Notes

Date	Departure	Arrival
Location		
Time		
Fuel		
Engine Hours		

Journey Summary			
Locks		Air Temp	
Swing Bridges		Wind	
Flow		Rain	

Waypoints & Stop-offs		
Location	Time	Notes

	Departure	Arrival
Date		
Location		
Time		
Fuel		
Engine Hours		

Journey Summary				
Locks		Air Temp		
Swing Bridges		Wind		
Flow		Rain		

Waypoints & Stop-offs		
Location	Time	Notes

Date	Departure	Arrival
Location		
Time		
Fuel		
Engine Hours		

Journey Summary			
Locks		Air Temp	
Swing Bridges		Wind	
Flow		Rain	

Waypoints & Stop-offs		
Location	Time	Notes

	Departure	Arrival
Date		
Location		
Time		
Fuel		
Engine Hours		

Journey Summary			
Locks		Air Temp	
Swing Bridges		Wind	
Flow		Rain	

Waypoints & Stop-offs		
Location	Time	Notes

	Departure	Arrival
Date		
Location		
Time		
Fuel		
Engine Hours		

Journey Summary

Locks		Air Temp	
Swing Bridges		Wind	
Flow		Rain	

Waypoints & Stop-offs

Location	Time	Notes

Date	Departure	Arrival
Location		
Time		
Fuel		
Engine Hours		

Journey Summary			
Locks		Air Temp	
Swing Bridges		Wind	
Flow		Rain	

Waypoints & Stop-offs		
Location	Time	Notes

	Departure	Arrival
Date		
Location		
Time		
Fuel		
Engine Hours		

Journey Summary			
Locks		Air Temp	
Swing Bridges		Wind	
Flow		Rain	

Waypoints & Stop-offs		
Location	Time	Notes

Date	Departure	Arrival
Location		
Time		
Fuel		
Engine Hours		

Journey Summary			
Locks		Air Temp	
Swing Bridges		Wind	
Flow		Rain	

Waypoints & Stop-offs		
Location	Time	Notes

Date	Departure	Arrival
Location		
Time		
Fuel		
Engine Hours		

Journey Summary			
Locks		**Air Temp**	
Swing Bridges		**Wind**	
Flow		**Rain**	

Waypoints & Stop-offs		
Location	Time	Notes

Date	Departure	Arrival
Location		
Time		
Fuel		
Engine Hours		

Journey Summary			
Locks		Air Temp	
Swing Bridges		Wind	
Flow		Rain	

Waypoints & Stop-offs		
Location	Time	Notes

Date	Departure	Arrival
Location		
Time		
Fuel		
Engine Hours		

Journey Summary			
Locks		Air Temp	
Swing Bridges		Wind	
Flow		Rain	

Waypoints & Stop-offs		
Location	Time	Notes

	Departure	Arrival
Date		
Location		
Time		
Fuel		
Engine Hours		

Journey Summary				
Locks		Air Temp		
Swing Bridges		Wind		
Flow		Rain		

Waypoints & Stop-offs		
Location	Time	Notes

Date	Departure	Arrival
Location		
Time		
Fuel		
Engine Hours		

Journey Summary			
Locks		Air Temp	
Swing Bridges		Wind	
Flow		Rain	

Waypoints & Stop-offs		
Location	Time	Notes

Date	Departure	Arrival
Location		
Time		
Fuel		
Engine Hours		

Journey Summary			
Locks		Air Temp	
Swing Bridges		Wind	
Flow		Rain	

Waypoints & Stop-offs		
Location	Time	Notes

	Departure	Arrival
Date		
Location		
Time		
Fuel		
Engine Hours		

Journey Summary			
Locks		Air Temp	
Swing Bridges		Wind	
Flow		Rain	

Waypoints & Stop-offs		
Location	Time	Notes

Date	Departure	Arrival
Location		
Time		
Fuel		
Engine Hours		

Journey Summary			
Locks		Air Temp	
Swing Bridges		Wind	
Flow		Rain	

Waypoints & Stop-offs		
Location	Time	Notes

	Departure	Arrival
Date		
Location		
Time		
Fuel		
Engine Hours		

Journey Summary			
Locks		Air Temp	
Swing Bridges		Wind	
Flow		Rain	

Waypoints & Stop-offs		
Location	Time	Notes

Date	Departure	Arrival
Location		
Time		
Fuel		
Engine Hours		

Journey Summary			
Locks		Air Temp	
Swing Bridges		Wind	
Flow		Rain	

Waypoints & Stop-offs		
Location	Time	Notes

Date	Departure	Arrival
Location		
Time		
Fuel		
Engine Hours		

Journey Summary				
Locks		Air Temp		
Swing Bridges		Wind		
Flow		Rain		

Waypoints & Stop-offs		
Location	Time	Notes

Date	Departure	Arrival
Location		
Time		
Fuel		
Engine Hours		

Journey Summary			
Locks		Air Temp	
Swing Bridges		Wind	
Flow		Rain	

Waypoints & Stop-offs		
Location	Time	Notes

	Departure	Arrival
Date		
Location		
Time		
Fuel		
Engine Hours		

Journey Summary			
Locks		Air Temp	
Swing Bridges		Wind	
Flow		Rain	

Waypoints & Stop-offs		
Location	Time	Notes

Date	Departure	Arrival
Location		
Time		
Fuel		
Engine Hours		

Journey Summary			
Locks		Air Temp	
Swing Bridges		Wind	
Flow		Rain	

Waypoints & Stop-offs		
Location	Time	Notes

	Departure	Arrival
Date		
Location		
Time		
Fuel		
Engine Hours		

Journey Summary			
Locks		Air Temp	
Swing Bridges		Wind	
Flow		Rain	

Waypoints & Stop-offs		
Location	Time	Notes

	Departure	Arrival
Date		
Location		
Time		
Fuel		
Engine Hours		

Journey Summary			
Locks		Air Temp	
Swing Bridges		Wind	
Flow		Rain	

Waypoints & Stop-offs		
Location	Time	Notes

Date	Departure	Arrival
Location		
Time		
Fuel		
Engine Hours		

Journey Summary			
Locks		Air Temp	
Swing Bridges		Wind	
Flow		Rain	

Waypoints & Stop-offs		
Location	Time	Notes

Date	Departure	Arrival
Location		
Time		
Fuel		
Engine Hours		

Journey Summary			
Locks		Air Temp	
Swing Bridges		Wind	
Flow		Rain	

Waypoints & Stop-offs		
Location	Time	Notes

	Departure	Arrival
Date		
Location		
Time		
Fuel		
Engine Hours		

Journey Summary			
Locks		Air Temp	
Swing Bridges		Wind	
Flow		Rain	

Waypoints & Stop-offs		
Location	Time	Notes

	Departure	Arrival
Date		
Location		
Time		
Fuel		
Engine Hours		

Journey Summary			
Locks		Air Temp	
Swing Bridges		Wind	
Flow		Rain	

Waypoints & Stop-offs		
Location	Time	Notes

Date	Departure	Arrival
Location		
Time		
Fuel		
Engine Hours		

Journey Summary			
Locks		Air Temp	
Swing Bridges		Wind	
Flow		Rain	

Waypoints & Stop-offs		
Location	Time	Notes

Date	Departure	Arrival
Location		
Time		
Fuel		
Engine Hours		

Journey Summary			
Locks		Air Temp	
Swing Bridges		Wind	
Flow		Rain	

Waypoints & Stop-offs		
Location	Time	Notes

Date	Departure	Arrival
Location		
Time		
Fuel		
Engine Hours		

Journey Summary			
Locks		Air Temp	
Swing Bridges		Wind	
Flow		Rain	

Waypoints & Stop-offs		
Location	Time	Notes

	Departure	Arrival
Date		
Location		
Time		
Fuel		
Engine Hours		

Journey Summary			
Locks		Air Temp	
Swing Bridges		Wind	
Flow		Rain	

Waypoints & Stop-offs		
Location	Time	Notes

Date	Departure	Arrival
Location		
Time		
Fuel		
Engine Hours		

Journey Summary			
Locks		**Air Temp**	
Swing Bridges		**Wind**	
Flow		**Rain**	

Waypoints & Stop-offs		
Location	Time	Notes

	Departure	Arrival
Date		
Location		
Time		
Fuel		
Engine Hours		

Journey Summary			
Locks		Air Temp	
Swing Bridges		Wind	
Flow		Rain	

Waypoints & Stop-offs		
Location	Time	Notes

Date	Departure	Arrival
Location		
Time		
Fuel		
Engine Hours		

Journey Summary			
Locks		Air Temp	
Swing Bridges		Wind	
Flow		Rain	

Waypoints & Stop-offs		
Location	Time	Notes

Date	Departure	Arrival
Location		
Time		
Fuel		
Engine Hours		

Journey Summary			
Locks		Air Temp	
Swing Bridges		Wind	
Flow		Rain	

Waypoints & Stop-offs		
Location	Time	Notes

Date	Departure	Arrival
Location		
Time		
Fuel		
Engine Hours		

Journey Summary			
Locks		**Air Temp**	
Swing Bridges		**Wind**	
Flow		**Rain**	

Waypoints & Stop-offs		
Location	Time	Notes

Date	Departure	Arrival
Location		
Time		
Fuel		
Engine Hours		

Journey Summary			
Locks		Air Temp	
Swing Bridges		Wind	
Flow		Rain	

Waypoints & Stop-offs		
Location	Time	Notes

Date	Departure	Arrival
Location		
Time		
Fuel		
Engine Hours		

Journey Summary			
Locks		Air Temp	
Swing Bridges		Wind	
Flow		Rain	

Waypoints & Stop-offs		
Location	Time	Notes

	Departure	Arrival
Date		
Location		
Time		
Fuel		
Engine Hours		

Journey Summary			
Locks		Air Temp	
Swing Bridges		Wind	
Flow		Rain	

Waypoints & Stop-offs		
Location	Time	Notes

Date	Departure	Arrival
Location		
Time		
Fuel		
Engine Hours		

Journey Summary			
Locks		Air Temp	
Swing Bridges		Wind	
Flow		Rain	

Waypoints & Stop-offs		
Location	Time	Notes

	Departure	Arrival
Date		
Location		
Time		
Fuel		
Engine Hours		

Journey Summary			
Locks		Air Temp	
Swing Bridges		Wind	
Flow		Rain	

Waypoints & Stop-offs		
Location	Time	Notes

Date	Departure	Arrival
Location		
Time		
Fuel		
Engine Hours		

Journey Summary			
Locks		Air Temp	
Swing Bridges		Wind	
Flow		Rain	

Waypoints & Stop-offs		
Location	Time	Notes

	Departure	Arrival
Date		
Location		
Time		
Fuel		
Engine Hours		

Journey Summary				
Locks		Air Temp		
Swing Bridges		Wind		
Flow		Rain		

Waypoints & Stop-offs		
Location	Time	Notes

Date	Departure	Arrival
Location		
Time		
Fuel		
Engine Hours		

Journey Summary			
Locks		Air Temp	
Swing Bridges		Wind	
Flow		Rain	

Waypoints & Stop-offs		
Location	Time	Notes

	Departure	Arrival
Date		
Location		
Time		
Fuel		
Engine Hours		

Journey Summary			
Locks		Air Temp	
Swing Bridges		Wind	
Flow		Rain	

Waypoints & Stop-offs		
Location	Time	Notes

Date	Departure	Arrival
Location		
Time		
Fuel		
Engine Hours		

Journey Summary			
Locks		Air Temp	
Swing Bridges		Wind	
Flow		Rain	

Waypoints & Stop-offs		
Location	Time	Notes

Notes:

Notes:

Notes:

Notes:

Notes:

Notes:

Notes:

Month:

Monday	Tuesday	Wednesday	Thursday	Friday	Saturday	Sunday

Month:

Monday	Tuesday	Wednesday	Thursday	Friday	Saturday	Sunday

Month:

Monday	Tuesday	Wednesday	Thursday	Friday	Saturday	Sunday

Month:

Monday	Tuesday	Wednesday	Thursday	Friday	Saturday	Sunday

Month:

Monday	Tuesday	Wednesday	Thursday	Friday	Saturday	Sunday

Month:

Monday	Tuesday	Wednesday	Thursday	Friday	Saturday	Sunday

Month:

Monday	Tuesday	Wednesday	Thursday	Friday	Saturday	Sunday

Month:

Monday	Tuesday	Wednesday	Thursday	Friday	Saturday	Sunday

Month:

Monday	Tuesday	Wednesday	Thursday	Friday	Saturday	Sunday

Month:

Monday	Tuesday	Wednesday	Thursday	Friday	Saturday	Sunday

Month:

Monday	Tuesday	Wednesday	Thursday	Friday	Saturday	Sunday

Month:

Monday	Tuesday	Wednesday	Thursday	Friday	Saturday	Sunday

Printed in Dunstable, United Kingdom